To Keep the Light Burning

Reflections in times of loss

Anne Le Marquand Hartigan

D1638257

salmon

Published in 2008 by
Salmon Poetry Ltd.,
Cliffs of Moher, County Clare, Ireland
Website: www.salmonpoetry.com
Email: info@salmonpoetry.com

ISBN 978-1-903392-96-6

Cover artwork: Batik by Anne Le Marquand Hartigan
Cover design & typesetting: Siobhán Hutson

For my mother who died too soon

Acknowledgments

Some of the poems in this volume have been previously published in the following poetry collections by Anne Le Marquand Hartigan:

Nourishment (Salmon Publishing, 2005): 'Care', 'Requiem for a Brother', 'The Kind Provider', and 'The Hawser'. The poem 'Care' is part of a film by Karen Westerlund, called *God, Smell and Her*, and is read in the film's soundtrack by the author.

Now is a Moveable Feast, Galway: Salmon Publishing (1991) : [The] 'Black Shed', 'Harvest', 'The Sister'.

Long Tongue, Dublin: Beaver Row Press (1982): 'Invisible Candles', 'Eternity is Now', 'Boundaries', 'Tides', 'La Pennelle', 'La Belle', 'Song'.

Return Single, Dublin: Beaver Row Press (1985): 'Elysium'

Immortal Sins, Dublin: Salmon Poetry/ Poolbeg (1993): 'Signals', 'Apples', 'Found', 'Fuel', 'A Flight of Birds', 'The Path of Enduring Knowledge'. 'The Path of Enduring Knowledge' was also published in The Field Day Anthology, Volume IV, Cork: Cork University Press (2002).

'The Hawser' was published in *The Clifden Anthology*, edited by Brendan Flynn, and published by Clifden Community Arts Week 2002.

Previously unpublished poems: 'Little Goddess', 'On the Burial of a Child', 'The Scattering of Ashes', 'Poem for a Cremation', 'The Seal', 'Dream'.

The publication of this book has been made possible by the generous financial support of Olivia Ward.

Contents

FOREWORD

by

Victoria Glendenning

I have known Anne Hartigan for many years – since our children were small and we were neighbours living just outside Dublin. Now we are Grandmothers.

How has that become this? It seems like yesterday. Yet in the interim we have known painful separation, bereavements, births, personal renewals, and yet more bereavements; and now it not only our friends who are in the front line against death, but ourselves.

Anne, as a poet, gets to grips with the life cycle and is comfortable with it. When we lose someone we love, we are out of our minds with grief and not well-placed to search the anthologies for words which will give our loss expression and some meaning. The comfort of religion may be no comfort at all; the traditional words are beautiful, but we do not believe them.

Neither do we want a sanitised procedure which makes no allowance for the enormity of our loss and grief.

The poems in this book will answer the need of all those many people who wish nowadays to create their own rituals for momentous occasions, whether a birth, a marriage or a death.

Anne, in her brief introduction to her poems, says all that is needed. I would add just one practical note. After the emotion of a loss and a funeral, however uplifting the funeral may be, one is left bereft and drained. Grieving, which goes on for a long time, is the most exhausting thing in the world. One never forgets, but one learns to live with one's memories. In the meanwhile, be good to yourself. Have a lot of rest and wait for the beginning of 'spring'.

Several of these poems have already found their way into the hearts of the bereaved, and have been found completely 'right'. It is great that they are now available to everyone.

VICTORIA GLENDINNING, CBE, is an award-winning biographer, novelist, critic and broadcaster. Among her many achievements, she won the James Tait Black Memorial Prize (for biography) and also the Duff Cooper Prize for *Rebecca West: A Life* (1987). She won the Whitbread Biography Award for both *Vita: A Life of V. Sackville-West* (1983) and *Trollope* (1992).

INTRODUCTION

by

Mark Patrick Hederman

I am surprised at how much I liked this book. It talks about death: your death, my death, the children's death, our mother's, our grandmother's death, without flinching. It gathers us around the emptiness and offers calm, truthful, reassuring words, 'human and comforting.' If it calls on God, it is 'Domestos. A comfy God:' It is not sentimental or sanctimonious; it is warm, down-to-earth, hopeful. 'This rice has a sweet calligraphy.' It is wrung from tearful experience, from battles fought. 'A new song,/ Born from the dark.'

Human beings have used words like charms to steady themselves on the brink of the abyss, 'flapping signals on the wind,' from *The Egyptian Book of the Dead*, over 3,000 years ago, to *The Book of Blessings* by John O'Donohue: 'Blessings/ To keep the light/ Burning.' Each one finds, or is given, their own particular talisman to hold, to trust. This book could be such a support for many.

There is something ancient and Celtic about these poems conveyed mostly through rhythm and repetition. 'Sound-music holds a magic.' It has the power of litanies and spells, 'signs charms and rubrics' in the poet's own words. They console as they beguile, 'a kind of charm, meant to ward off evil, give protection.' For this poet 'Dying is love. Very practical.' And echoing St Paul and The Song of Songs she emphatically affirms that 'Love does conquer death.' So, if you are living in a time of loss yourself, or if you need words to accompany you on that fateful journey in the tumbril towards the guillotine, ultimately the fate of each one of us, you could do worse than have Anne Le Marquand Hartigan whispering in your ear: 'Leaving is a dying art/ necessary to begin.'

Mark Patrick Hederman OSB Monk at Glenstal Abbey, County Limerick, Ireland

To Keep the Light Burning

Reflections in times of loss

I saw a dead person for the first time at around the age of ten. An aunt took me to a home in the village, to pay our respects to a family who had lost a relative. We were taken into the room where the dead woman was laid out in her bed, candles at her head and feet. We prayed, gave our sympathies to the mourning family, then left again. We had completed what was then the common custom.

This happened in Ireland, when my mother and I were home from England on a visit. When I returned to England, I was the only one in my class who had ever seen a dead person. I felt proud and unique; I knew I was fortunate in some way. My friends were awestruck and very curious. I think they envied me.

That I remember this experience so clearly shows it had a profound effect. It was not at all frightening, but memorable and strange. To see the dead is a less and less common experience.

In the past and sometimes still today, the dead would lie in their own home until they made the final journey to the graveyard. There, they would be visited and 'waked' with music, song and drink. This 'waking the dead' is an ancient task. Accompanying our dead on their journey from this life to the next, but also accompanying ourselves as we acclimatise to our loss.

The old customs provided help and sustenance. The visitors to the house would often bring food for the bereaved family. These visits gave practical support as well as showing solidarity with the bereaved – all very helpful in the move towards healing.

At funerals in the past, the men of the family would carry the coffin on their shoulders to the graveside, then after the final prayers or oration, they would fill in the grave with earth in front of our eyes. This practice still happens today in some places – so no need for that bit of artificial grass spread over the mound of clay, disguising nothing.

In most parts of Ireland, it would be customary to say a decade of the Rosary in Irish or English. After that, everyone would depart for a much-needed hearty meal, laced with glasses of whisky. We bury our dead well in Ireland, and I have heard it said that some would prefer a good funeral, to a wedding, any day!

It is worth thinking about these ways of the past, to see how their spirit might be reinstated in the places where present-day formalities have taken death away from the family, and dehumanised them. Funeral parlours are in Ireland as elsewhere now, and they can and do fulfil a function. But it is good to consider that they are not the only option, and might not be the best one.

Religions have, over the centuries, developed rituals that provide a path for people to travel towards an acceptance of death, a form through which we can channel grief. Today, some of us do not feel part of any religion. Many more live without formal practice. So we can be left without a ready-made ritual to call on.

It is the nature of life to be constantly changing, so our rituals may be out of step with life as we live it now. Ceremonies happen at crematoria, in gardens, in homes. Families bring the ashes of their dead to many different places. They scatter them in the countryside, on the sea, or take them by plane across the world. We are inventing our own rituals and searching for new words to help us express our grief and find some consolation.

This universal need for ritual and ceremony was one of the reasons I wrote this book. A poem itself is a ritual: the formal expression of strong and passionate emotions distilled and shaped by form. Poetry is the music of the word. Both poetry and music arouse the emotions, consoling us and providing us with a method of expressing feelings at critical times. Dealing with the experience of death is certainly a critical period. We have to come to terms with and accept grief, feel and express it, and then find a way to move on. Not weakened but, with the passing of time, perhaps even strengthened by our loss.

This is not easy to achieve. At times it may seem impossible. However, we are all going to be faced with this situation at some time in our lives, facing others', and ultimately our own, death.

There is also a personal reason why I put this book together. In August 2001 I suffered the sudden and unexpected loss of an important friend. I read the poems 'Care' and 'The Black Shed' at his funeral service, which took place in a sunny garden in England. Then a day or two later, after I had returned home to Ireland, the appalling horror of September 11th was hurled upon us. One loss ricocheted onto the other. Here in Ireland we all grieved with America. Many of us had direct connections with those who lost family and friends, or who had narrow escapes. Almost everyone in Ireland was directly affected. We held a day of national mourning, and wondered would the world ever be the same again. These two griefs became the force and energy that fuelled the making of this book.

The way in which we honour the dead is a mark of civilization. Death is part of life; we cannot escape it. How we deal with it has a great bearing on how we live. To feel grief, to be able to express it positively, can help us to heal and move on. We need to express our sorrow, to show our respect and love, to honour the unique quality of the person who has gone.

The poems in this book have been chosen for their aptness at a time of loss, to be read aloud at a funeral service or in private. I have myself read some of these poems at the funerals of friends and family, and this privilege has also been helpful to me personally.

So, with the hope that these poems might meet a need, become a starting point, help with the forming of a new ritual or be included in an old one, or just read privately, I make this small book.

ANNE LE MARQUAND HARTIGAN
November 2008

THE BLACK SHED

It may seem strange to open this book with a poem about a birth, but to me it has a logic to it. Birth is natural, as is death. Facing birth, facing death, are life's two absolutes.

The birth of creatures, human or animal, is always moving. I had a lovely experience with my youngest child when he was about two. He ran into our bedroom early one morning crying out: "Mummy! Mummy! The cat's had mice!" The kittens had been born on the bottom of his bed.

There is a necessity to choose good places for certain acts. Animals, if they are allowed, choose their own good places to give birth. It is said cows and mares usually calve or foal down on a blind spring. I know that, when having my own children, nothing felt more unnatural to me than going into hospital when I was in labour, leaving my own safe nest to move into such an alien environment. Fortunately I did manage to have my fifth child at home in my own bed and the peace, simplicity and ease was unbelievable, especially the other four children coming to see the baby a few minutes after she was born.

'The Black Shed' connects us back to the land – the land that is full of heart – and to a particular little field called the Black Shed. This field was always permanent pasture as it was small and oddly shaped, and therefore, with modern machinery, difficult to plough. So it tended to be the one into which we put our calving cows – though in this poem, it is our mare giving birth to her first foal.

The horse is one of the few large animals that we come in contact with these days and even this is becoming rare for many of us. To stand by a horse allows us to feel our own size. (Our true size?) In the presence of a horse, I feel the comfort of being in proportion. When we live in cities, everything is made to our measure, under our control, to suit us, the human species; this gives us a warped view of our importance.

A woman phoned me with the request that she might read 'The Black Shed' at her father's funeral. She told me she had heard it read by a priest at a graveside in the west of Ireland. Maybe we need the confirmation and beauty of birth when we face the stark fact of death.

The Black Shed

The black shed
is gone now,
tumbled down
fifty years ago
or more, but the name
stands.

A little field
too awkward
to plough, uneven-
shaped, but sheltered
with high hedges
and flaring furze; soon
early bite grows quick,
before milk-easing June.

Here mares
foal down,
and many a heifer
heaved her young to earth.

A good place for birth.

Our first time ever foal
was dropped there,
one night in a sudden wild,
a summer storm.

Small Dermot rushed
the early morning news

                                  but we

had felt her coming
in the wind's wet knocking.

Up and over
daylight
lane and field
we went
in the well-washed morning;

homed, by the hedge
the mare, contented, fat
sat back, like a dog
on her haunches.

And this new chocolate life
a clean licked
catkin creature

                      Stood,

Strut up;

High – headed as her dam
(suede nostrils flickering
our hands our faces),
and noticed all this New,

O jade
O jewel,

This morning's miracle.

CARE

A Charm

In the writing of 'Care', I use a particular form that is found in early Irish poetry, poetry written in the Irish language. I don't speak Irish myself, as I was reared in England, so I have only read this vibrant poetry in translation, but it has had a profound influence on my work.

Early Irish poetry has strong visual imagery and I love the use of repetition for both its power and its beauty. In 'Care', the repetition of 'you' places full emphasis on the person, the loved one – the loved and lost one.

Repetitions are used in litanies, and in the prayer of the Rosary. It is close to the idea of a spell, the creating of magic by words – which is surely the aim of the poet? So this poem is a kind of charm, meant to ward off evil, give protection.

This poem sparked the making of this collection. The first time I read 'Care' was at the funeral of a long-time and loved friend, who had died suddenly and tragically while speaking on the phone to her husband. She was only in her fifties. Later her husband had three lines from this poem inscribed on the headstone of her grave:

Keep all harm from you
For this night for you
Dream of light for you

It was he who suggested to me, after her funeral, that I make a book of poetry to be read at the time of a burial. Poems that might provide the basis of new rituals for those going through loss.

'Care' is a poem of love. It can be said for the one who has gone and for those who are left – whether or not you have a belief in a God. Through it, we wish those we love all goodness and comfort: the dead and the living. All of us need blessings.

Care

A Charm

This my prayer.

This my prayer for you
This light day for you

Pray for you
God's hand for you

Stand for you

The green land for you
The wet grass for you
Swallow's wing for you
The sea's sand for you
The rock's strength for you
The tree's song for you
Thistledown for you

Silence for you
Cloud for you
Rain for you
No pain for you
No hurt befall you
A kind step for you
A soft word for you
What have I kept for you
In my heart for you
I will not part for you
Treasure kept for you

Warm for you
Away from storm for you
No alarm for you
Keep all harm from you
For this night for you
Dream of light for you

This my charm for you

For this day for you
This I pray for you

This my prayer.

INVISIBLE CANDLES

The idea of a journey or a passage leading to a different life, a changed place or a changed self, is part of many religions and philosophies: death is seen as a necessary stage in a person's development. For Christians death leads to the home called Heaven, and this, for those who follow the Christian way of life, is a certainty.

Not all share this certainty about an afterlife, but the death of a close other can be part of our own journey. Certainly, it will change us. Perhaps we are being given a chance to gain from this experience. I do know those close to me help me at these times. They light those invisible candles, or they themselves are my invisiable candles.

It is such a common experience to suffer depression that it seems to be an inescapable part of the human condition, and maybe a necessary part. I am thinking of Saint Teresa of Avila and Saint John of the Cross, who lived in Spain in the same period and knew each other. When they met and talked, they could not see each other face to face since Saint Teresa, in her reforms of the Carmelite Order, had imposed the strict rule of isolation, and she was concealed behind a grille. It is said that as they talked they would both levitate, so intense was their response to their conversation on spiritual matters.

Many saints like these two expect and accept that they will have to go through a time when they lose all hope and faith, and feel only 'the black' creeping upon them. They called this state 'the dark night of the soul'.

This phrase gives a different and more creative feeling than the word depression, which is a word without activity or energy. The mystics thought of the dark night of the soul as an essential passage leading to a new level of enlightenment, one that could not be reached without making a dark and difficult journey.

Think also of the many fairy stories and folk tales where the hero or heroine has to go through harsh trials, perform impossible feats, before obtaining their heart's desire.

I wrote this poem when my husband was far away travelling, and I was going through a barren time. The writing of a poem is one way a poet works to make sense of life for herself, to light her own candle, to enable her to see.

A poet was traditionally a seer, one who looks for, and then presents us with a vision, a light. Without the dark, we cannot see the flame. The seed needs the fecund dark in order to grow towards the light. Perhaps we do too.

Invisible Candles

You may have been
The traveller

But I have been
On some dark journey,
Only now the way
Clearing a little.

This time I stood
Without you

When the black
Came in the window
And sat at the foot
Of my bed

In the back of my head
As the black cat would
With his fellow...

No shooing
Was effective

But this scribbler
Made signs
Charms and rubrics

Blessings
To keep the light
Burning.

There must be
Invisible candles
Alight for us
When we least know it

Blessed
For those in dark corners.

REQUIEM FOR
A BROTHER

I wrote this for a friend who lost a younger brother. Neither of these men were young, but at any age it is hard enough to lose a brother. To lose one younger than yourself goes against natural expectation, and our own foundations are shaken. Our families stand around us, like encircling standing stones, even if we do not see them often or do not like them or get on with them. As long as they remain there, we still feel safe.

This friend of mine spoke warmly about his brother, whom I had never met. So my knowledge of the brother came from my friend's joyous stories of the man's humanity, his words spilling out spontaneously as he faced his own loss. The need to talk about the person who has gone is universal. To talk this way is good. We are storing details of the person, so as to put a true imprint of them indelibly into our brains. This continual talking and repeating of stories about the person we have lost is a great healer.

It is easy to be afraid that we will not remember how they looked, that they will somehow slip from our grasp. I remember fearing that I would not be able to remember my mother's face. Even now, I have a difficulty in seeing her clearly in my mind's eye. Photos are never the face we want to hold; we want some expression that summed up the person to us, maybe not even a real expression. We want to remember smell, and feel, and touch.

So, this is a poem talking about the man gone, who was close to his family and who had a mischievous sense of fun.

Requiem For A Brother

Your brother has not left
he is around the place –

he has just gone
outside for a while

he'll be back
he has a joke to tell you.

He's saying he's off
that there is somewhere to visit

but he's not leaving really,
it's not possible, you're brothers.

He's talking to your
     mother
and giving your father
     a hand
he's talking to himself
     as you do.

This is time for him
to do other things – go home

for a while, sort things out,
see the neighbours

but he'll be here.
He'll keep a sweet eye on his wife

and you will hear him laugh
now and then

when he drops in
to share secrets with you –

and remind you, he's
still up to mischief.

ETERNITY IS NOW

I think we still believe that love conquers death, for love contains hope. When we face the death of someone we love, we face the fact that the physical presence of that person is going, has gone, and we have no choice but to let them go. So we hold on to what is left: memory, love and respect.

The form of this poem was a way of capturing the spiralling of emotions when you are in love: how you can swing from highs to lows in a wonderful ecstatic movement. Our emotions swing just as violently when we feel loss, but we have to remember that this is natural too. It is this way only because we have loved. It is completely human. So *eternity is now*, when and where we love. Love *does* conquer death.

Ways of commemorating our loved ones will inevitably change now that so many of us do not bury our dead in the earth, but scatter their ashes to the winds, at sea or on land. There will be no stone carved with a name to remain for the generations to come and visit. I can still go to the family graves of my mother's and father's families, which go back to the seventeen hundreds. Is this now going to be a thing of the past?

In some parts of Ireland there used to be an old way of making a proposal of marriage, it went like this: the man said, "Would you be buried with my people?" This seems humourous to us now, but it meant joining with another's family and becoming a part of that family. Family gravestones carry family history.

If we don't have gravestones, we will have to invent new ways of holding the past with us. Poetry can help us here. And song. Words and music passed from mouth to mouth. But I am inclined to think we still like the idea of a stone with names carved upon it. There is some primitive satisfaction from seeing the name carved in stone; it gives the feeling of permanence and strength. We feel it will last after we have gone. We all hope for some form of immortality.

Eternity Is Now

Eternity Is now

because I love;

so swing, precarious

as fragile birds

above,
                a string,
am hanging
                by a thread
between,
                the light,
the dark,
                hovering
        to plunge,
        dive,
                spring
from joy
                to pain,
spiralling
                back again
to sing;

Eternity is now

because I love.

ELYSIUM

Perhaps at the time of the greatest loss, it is the time to remember our greatest bliss, its unity and magic. Bliss is not a state that remains, but neither, luckily, is grief. Bliss, that Elysium, is not something we can consciously look or plan for. We do create it, but not by working for it. It comes as a gift.

This poem celebrates a very particular time in my life, a magic few days in a simple but beautiful house away in the country, when the snow came down and buried us in white. We were shut off from the world in warmth and in that beautiful silence that falls on the world with the coming of snow. We were snowed in, snowed into, a few days of peace and perfection.

Elysium – also called the Elysian Fields – was the ancient Greeks' name for the abode after death of the brave and good and also for them and us a place or a state of ideal happiness.

When we suffer the greatest loss it is time to remember the opposite, so that we can sing and celebrate the positive in life. This can give us hope: by going through the loss we are enabled to sing again 'a new song, / born from the dark'.

Elysium

I have been to Elysium.

There are no maps to find it.
No marks on trees.

Nothing easy or difficult
Along the way to show you,

You cannot plan or strain
Put away all ideas of an
Organised expedition.

It is no good squeezing the eyesight
To try and see in the distance.

Love is dangerous.
Danger on its every needle.

Calculations and ideas are out of order,
Nothing wild or heroic or fine minded, No

Revolutions with bristling pistols
No overturning tables, this,

Is all slow motion.

But now the revolving round
Moon and Sun and through them

Swinging on lazy swings
Of snow and firelight,

Down long low loops
Words and whispers

An O of music
For us to rest in.

A new song,
Born from the dark.

BOUNDARIES

The marking of boundaries is a basic human activity and there is no surer boundary than that between the living and the dead. An aunt of mine lived to the great age of ninety-six. Even at that age, death seemed unnatural.

She was a devout and vigorous Catholic, a clear-headed and loving woman. I was determined she would have as comfortable a passing as could be managed. My aunt's belief in the next world was total. During her last weeks she pushed away the rosary beads when a nurse put them in her hands, and said, "I have done all my praying". She was a practical person. She was quite right: she had.

After her death, my cousin and I would joke that we had not had a postcard from her yet, to tell us how she was getting on in heaven. This joke had a weird wish in it. We wanted a sign that life is not this brief, inconclusive span. That there is something more, and if someone as positive and convinced about heaven as she, was *not* going to send us a message, well, who would?

In the country in Ireland the old custom was to white-wash cottages and walls in the springtime, before Easter came. This signified both the new life of spring and the resurrection of Christ. In the village at home bound-aries were sometimes marked by stones, and these too were whitewashed. (Mind you, they would also be pushed outwards, surreptitiously, in order to gain a little more land.)

There are boundaries between the living and the living and – invincibly – between the living and the dead. Why, we just don't know. Boundaries can be necessary for our security, to feel safe, to know where we are, where we belong.

Boundaries

There is a boundary between
Your land, my land.

High rough hedges growing carelessly,
Or long stone walls,
Whitened every spring.

The border stones are numbered
One by one, edged over sometimes
Better to gather in
One more green yard.

So we mark our outsides,
Guard our in.

I know my hedge is weakened,
There are gaps
Propped with old bedsteads
And the stranded wire,

I can see your greenness shining in.
Your well-stocked pastures
Hold a growing sheen.

So I would push the willow stems apart,
Pull at those thorns, tie back
The old wire strand,
Break down the boundaries that

Stand between
Your land, my land.

TIDES

It seems to me that it took me an unnaturally long time to realise that life is change. I always expected things to stay the same, but that is the last thing on earth that is going to happen. Walk on the beach, and see the sea moving the sand and washing it into that incredible, clean newness, each shell lying there in breathtaking freshness. You know your footprint is the first. It's a similar magic when you open a spiky horse-chestnut fruit, and know that yours are the first eyes to see the glossy new conker within, the seed of a tree.

Perfection is just not part of being human. Still, there lie the sea and sand: they shine in their ever-changing movement and flow, they are perfection in our eyes. Such sights, sounds and smells refresh us, open a necessary space in the mind. We are driven to find this kind of space when we face the large events in our lives. In that space, we can see more sharply. We can see with clearness.

The tides rise and fall with predictable rhythm, they keep their own regular time. The marking of time is important to us, and it is a popular cliché that time heals. Like most clichés, it has some truth in it. Another custom in Ireland in the Catholic tradition is the 'Month's Mind', when Mass is celebrated for the one who has died, exactly a month after their death. When friends and family come together again to pray and remember the dead person just one month on, this is human and comforting. This Month's Mind Mass marks the day when a most difficult time has passed, showing us that time that can travel so slowly, *does* pass and does move us on.

Tides

The water washed your name
    away from the sand; nothing holds:
Look at this changing, each day
    wears a fresh smell, carrying

Old odours with it. We continue
    despite the rise and fall of the sea.
Its lace wiping the slate an imaginary
    clean. Footprint it, there

Again we have carved in
    the old weakness, the old pain
On the new sheen. The sands
    pull, pull underfoot back to the sea

Obeying their own deep order.
    While you rise gull sharp in my mind;
The shell lies perfectly empty.
    The waves pound and pound.

LA PENNELLE

'La Pennelle' was written in an old farmhouse in France where I was on holiday with my family.

There was a huge summer storm, and afterwards there was a sudden moist stillness. A silence, as if the whole countryside was holding its breath, a pause when the atmosphere itself made us still.

After experiencing the passion of grief, the turmoil and tussle to reject the reality of loss, we need a place like this to draw breath and find solace. To re-gather strength. To take life on again. So a simple poem about country-side after summer rain can mirror what we are feeling, and offer us the hope that by moving through grief we can arrive at a peaceful place, ready to go on with life as it is.

La Pennelle

After rain, things clear.

Although the soft hills
Lie dumb in the rising mist,
And over the hanging barley
Swifts curve and twist
Letters into the moist air.

Birds sing back the sun,
Now no blasting,
Only poppies scream, but muted,
Wet washing.

We need gentling,
The winds are not around.
Insects are out;
Grass head and butterflies
Patterning; something

Is being born.

LA BELLE

This poem was written on the same holiday in France, in the house called La Pennelle. The French themselves speak of France as 'La Belle France' – Beautiful France. They love their country as we do ours, but how lovely to address it so elegantly.

At La Pennelle we had a wonderful holiday. The house had spacious rooms with old tiled floors cool and comforting to bare feet in the heat. I remember seeing in one of those tiles the imprint of two tiny cat paws. So some little cat had jumped on these tiles as they dried before being baked, and this small animal had left its mark there for all eternity – well, for as long as this already very old floor lasts.

We do turn to the natural world when we are full of emotion. Plants, trees, mountains, water, birds, all profoundly affect our feelings and we use them to connect with our deepest emotions: it is easier and often clearer to express ourselves that way. Also it moves us out, out of our own self-obsession, into the freedom of the universe. To turn broodingly inward will not lead to refreshment.

'La Belle' is frankly a celebration of the good things of this life. When we say goodbye to someone who had the gift of wholehearted enjoyment, we want, in our mourning of them, to celebrate them the way they were. To delight in their gift for living which they, quite naturally, shared with us. Such a person spreads contagious joy and we know how lucky we have been to know them, and how much they have lit up our life with energy and humour.

This poem that celebrates life and sexuality may also appeal to those who do not follow the Christian god, but lean towards more pagan beliefs.

La Belle

These hills roll and trees
    Christen the contours.

What goddess slept here,
    What cheerful nights
Did she spend spilling
    Blessings in the brown earth?

The snake, earth colours twists
    From the sun, his coils
Stretching a reach of warmth;
    Here all grows:

Sweetness oozes, lines of vines
    Deline the hills, sun
And moon rise and fall
    Holding hands.

Each acre is goodness;
    Red and white
The wine flows.

SIGNALS

There is a need for a place where we can retreat and lick our wounds, not be adventurous, be *home*. A safe and unpretentious place. A familiar place, that supports us and feeds us with the ordinary, which is neither dramatic nor beautiful, and may be old and untidy, rather like ourselves. Home is a place where we are not on show. It is from here that, when we have recovered, by just letting things be, letting time pass, we will dare again to face the outside world. Then, like the washing on the line, we signal we are ready to take the outside life on again.

I wrote this poem while I and my family lived in a rented house by the sea. The house was on a road of similar and not particularly attractive houses, and the furniture and the decoration was not chosen by us. To my surprise I found this a kind of relief. I was not responsible for the colour of the walls, and the ancient sofa was nothing to do with me. It gave me a freedom to get on with my painting and writing and not care. Neither I nor my husband would be expecting the other to mend this or fix that. That was the landlord's responsibility, not ours. We both found this casual way of going about things a happy release.

In day-to-day living we accept the spaces we make for ourselves, and what is familiar is comforting. Recovering from loss is not a time to go out and brave the world; we can retreat and cuddle up by the fire if that is what we want to do. It is a time when you can leave responsibilities to others, and mind just ourselves.

'Signals' might also celebrate someone who appreciated homemaking in a particular way, a person who was a real homemaker. This is a great art and only some have it. They seem to do it naturally without any particular effort, and they spread a special comfort into our lives.

Signals

I speak with simple things
The tongues of teacups
Peel curl of potato
This rice has a sweet calligraphy.

Here is my hermit's home,
Domestos. A comfy God.

Holding all necessities.
Full belly, warm hearth.

The language of the kettle
And the sagging chair
Reassure as old friends do;
To breathe other adventurous

Air, is not needed. This
Is decent, like a white
Teacloth spread gaily as washing
Flapping signals, on the wind.

APPLES

I always enjoy speaking this poem at readings, probably because it is rhyming and simply rhythmic, so is comforting to recite. The sounds are soothing. Then autumn is such a lovely season when all the growth halts, waits, while we are busy harvesting: the natural world has finished its work, and is still.

One of the reasons that poetry is so suitable for important occasions is because of the power of its rhythms, its word-music, giving a power that prose seldom processes. This very sound-music holds a magic and conveys the emotions of the poem even if the words are not fully taken in with a first hearing.

So this is a comforting poem, offering the sort of simple comfort described in the line 'curved as arms around a child': a child who loves you, and welcomes being freely wrapped in your arms. As adults we do not express ourselves so naturally or freely, and we are the worse off because of it.

The rhythm of the poem is the pattern of this movement, of continuing life that carries us on its flow, eases us on into life. In accepting this we acknowledge that leaving can be part of a new beginning.

Apples

September is a harbouring time
  curved as arms around a child
as round the apples of the world
  drawing in and laying down
resting in the resting place.

Finding shelter, find repose
  store on shelves for winter's needs
time moves quietly to a close
  as the mists dissolve by breeze

as the clouds disperse by light
  as the water breaks to foam
as the twilight sinks to night
  as the moon that is full blown.

Slowly trees present their bones
  shed, are stark, gaunt and grim,
      leaving is a dying art
      necessary to begin.

BORDER

Gardens play such a big part in so many people's lives. We remember people for their love of gardens. Gardens are enjoyed all through life, and cross all barriers of race, age, and class. Gardens enchant, spread delight, and spread this delight from generation to generation.

I was staying with my oldest and closest friend, Rose. She and I were at school together, and knew each other's mothers well. Her mother was a keen gardener and knew all the plants and their Latin names.

The evening was dull, bleak; typical November. Rose was creating a new large flower border. The only dash of colour was that of the fallen cherry leaves. I watched her as she was putting in these unimpressive little plants, giving me all their amazing Latin names. I was struck by the powerful continuity we held together, through plants, friendship, language and our mothers. All those different ways of growing. The poetry of it.

Border

for Rose

You knew all the names for plants
as your mother did.   And explained
bending to the dark November soil
showing me a small green, or a brown
straggle of stalk clasping the earth,
which was which.

           Your fingers rooted,
pressing the young plants in;   here,
here and here.   I kick bright cherry leaves
listening to your litany of Latin.   Still names,
growing in a dead language.

FOUND

Sometimes, something is under your nose and you just do not see it. This can happen with friendship. You do not realise how important a person is until something highlights it, and like a flash of light all things seem startlingly clear, almost like a vision. We hope that we do not have to wait until someone dies to know how important he or she was in our lives.

I think it happens more often than we think, that a friendship has suddenly turned head over heels, and is suddenly more and different. It is a love affair; it is pure and simply love at second sight. And this poem celebrates this discovery of love and the deep blessing of such a find.

Found

Dug with my spade
parted the soft turf
to find treasure.

No dim gold.
No hard diamond.
No bone ivory.

Although it has rested
under my feet since
the beginning of a time,

if it was brightening rubies
it would say nothing, just
be valuable and useless.

I see it, gleaming and warm
as a gold skull
resting in depths, un-disturbably.

I sang its songs often
not knowing its existence,
but it knew, being under my feet
and bearing me up.

Now I grasp
and recognise newness and oldness,
and what it is to be called blessed.

THE PATH OF ENDURING
KNOWLEDGE

I was visiting the hot springs in Rotorua, New Zealand, walking by a stream that is now on the tourist trail, and discovering as I walked that this was a place of pilgrimage, a holy place for the Maori people. There, walking on my own, I was overcome by the significance of the place. The name of the stream was written in Maori, and translated into English as 'The Path of Enduring Knowledge'. The power of that name struck deep.

Water is by its nature holy. However, this stream was even more special and unusual, for the water that flowed fast and vigorously was boiling. The path led on and up, to a pool, a bubbling well so beautiful that it made me gasp. It was round and of a brilliant azure colour, surrounded by pure white rock. Bubbles were rising to the surface of the hot water. Standing by this holy well, on the other side of the world from Ireland, I thought of standing by a most perfect round Holy Well in Tipperary.

This Irish well, its icy water translucent and green, is surrounded by banks of green soft turf and there's an ash tree growing beside it. A stream flows from the well, and into the freezing water we had walked barefoot, our ankles nearly cut from us with the cold. Now, here, on the other side of the world, I found the very opposite: holy hot water – and the complete and stunning link between the two.

That a stream is a path of enduring knowledge encourages thoughts to rise and flow, like the stream itself. That these ancient places of pilgrimage still hold truths for us. That knowledge, like water, does endure. That our endurance of a difficult time will – can, must – open possibilities. And that these can lead us to wisdom.

The divining rod is still used to discover where water runs underground. My husband taught himself to divine for water and sank a well in a field where there was no water for the cattle. Then he found all the old drains in one field on the farm, drains my grandfather had laid a hundred years ago, and this enabled the men to find the outlets long buried. When they dug down in the ditches to clear these outlets, out ran the water sweet and clear.

The Path of Enduring Knowledge

It is a path we are all on:
we cannot change it,
whatever way you step
knowledge keeps knocking you.

There is no way to avoid it,
so travel easy
take care
safe journey.

If you stood immobile
at the sink all day
you are still on it.
Shutting the eyes is useless,
I know all this
and yet know nothing, but

the old ways of pilgrimage
have sound founding, and
our ancestors are waving to us
up through the ever bubbling spring,
in the warm stones underfoot, and,
in that startle of azure water,
that white rock.

FUEL

We seem to spend our lives trying to make sense of things. Nowadays many of us are without the certainty of a life after death that our ancestors believed in – or so we like to think. They may have had as many doubts as we do. Their lives were often shorter and harder, and the harder it is to survive, the less time there is for introspection. We may feel that when we die that is the end. This has a comfortable simplicity. It removes a continual responsibility.

The poem 'Fuel' asks the question: do we invent the idea of heaven in order to try to make sense of the vicissitudes of life? Does love survive everything, all the different loves in our lives, the men and women, the children with their wonderful differences? Somehow love seems to survive even when we are not at all aware, and to burst forth for us again when we least expect it.

Fuel

i

Heaven is necessary as an epilogue,
to make sense of all this? This love,
given – away, or left in the dust, love?
Mostly clumsiness, we don't mean to waste it;
the cruelties, so small and mean.

Somewhere else saints fly up in ecstasy.
Here, I turn to your pale body, mostly
absent, mostly in my mind,
mostly a dream,
mostly

and remember holding my third child
how he would grip his legs riding my hip
and how his toy dog was very important.

ii

What is important lives quite on its own
breathing in and out
without measuring anything, letting

love flow over grass, flowers, pavements,
lying there for feet
tarmac and wheels pressing: love

can go on without a lover to receive,
without lips, without body,
its taste waiting, so, when touch meets touch,
all fires burn more deeply.

A FLIGHT OF BIRDS

Sometimes it is not necessary to do anything. Just let things happen, give way to the moment.

Migrating birds come to Ireland and Britain in spring and again in the autumn, and each time I am caught up in the excitement of these visitors flying in over the estuary of the river Boyne, near my family home.

Here the sky is huge and the birds sweep and twist in vast flocks, all moving in a thrilling dance, as if they were one. The sight of them is breathtaking and magnificent. We are so heavy, anchored to earth. When we watch birds, our spirit lifts off with them, into another space. We can take this leap, this move, and fly.

We hope that our dead take off into some kind of flight, into lightness, a place of joy.

The childish idea that heaven is always up there above the clouds stays in our imaginations. As a small child I thought this, and felt it would be very difficult to walk in clouds when I got to heaven, and that my feet would sink in, and it would be as hard as walking in soft sand.

As a child I could fly in my dreams. I managed to control my nightmares by jumping into the air, but it was hard work to fly away and escape from my pursuers. To gain the air in the joy of flight is the opposite to feeling the heaviness of the body, and the pull of gravity. The dream of flight is to take off into another world.

A Flight of Birds

I don't have to do anything
about the birds dropping down
from the sky,

they will do it anyway
without our knowledge
of their pattern.

A shape, a movement
that twists my spirit
and gives me lift, fly,
somehow more air
in the body,

this solidity I lose
for a small second,
the birds catch me up
in their power to leave

I am flown then.

SONG

It was only years after writing 'Song' that I saw why I had written it. It is a poem about taking a step towards change, having completed duties that demanded to be done, fulfilled responsibilities that were required, and then to move on towards a new life.

The American poet Adrienne Rich says about writing poetry, "we write what we do not know we know". In 'Song' I was telling myself and my long dead mother that I was about to live my life my own way, that the inherited rules I received from her were not going to hold me any longer, that I was going to step out and live by my own rules.

Interestingly, I do remember this poem was written not long after the death of one of my mother's sisters. Death can release us from influences that control us without our really being aware of them. Death can open us up to a new freedom.

Song

Mother untie my apron strings
And hang it on the door,
For I have washed the dishes,
And I have swept the floor,

I've smoothed my hair down carefully
And there is nothing more,
But the ring around the moon tonight
Is playing on the floor.

It's singing in my head tonight
It's dancing in my eyes,
There's spinning in my mind tonight
Whirled by seabirds' cries.

I've lit a little lamp, my love,
It's burning in my mind,
The door is creeping open
I'm lifting up the blind.

I have undone my apron strings
It's fallen to the floor,
The moon has winked her eye at me,
My hand is on the door.

THE HAWSER

Separation is so much part of life that it has been the subject of love songs throughout the ages. We keep on singing and writing about it, the pain and the passionate, pleasurable, ache of lovers parted, and on it goes…

A hawser is a strong rope fastened to the bow (front) of a boat. As the boat comes into harbour, the hawser is thrown to someone on shore, or one of the boat's crew who is holding the hawser jumps ashore. The hawser is tied, or 'made fast', to a ring or bollard so as to secure the boat. Then another hawser is taken from the stern (rear) of the boat and secured in a similar fashion.

'The Hawser' is, of course, a love poem; and the good feeling of a man's heavy arm, thrown across his lover in his relaxed sleep, is like the heavy weight of the hawser itself. We throw lines to each other across life, and out into the unknown beyond this life. This is what a poet attempts to do with words, continually throwing out a line, testing its strengths and hoping it falls where it will be heard, and that it will connect us one to another, and to ourselves.

The Hawser

Throwing a Line

In the deep pause of night
I can think of you
heavy-limbed and lying

turn to me across the ocean
throw out an arm
let its weight fall across me

as a rope from boat to shore.

LITTLE GODDESS

The Burren is a place with strange magical, moon-like mountains in County Clare on the west coast of Ireland. Thirty years ago, this place was almost unknown to tourists: to arrive there was like walking on the moon.

Here you can find one of the many 'Sheela-na-Gigs' that hide all over Ireland. A Sheela-na-Gig is a stone carving of a female goddess. She turns up again and again on the walls of ancient churches and other buildings. She is usually a small, naked, quite crude figure, her ribs distinctly showing. She holds her vulva open, or points to it. There are many examples in the National Museum of Ireland, but because of her frank display of her sex, they are not on general view. She is often regarded these days as a vital, strong, goddess figure. This poem is to celebrate the Sheela-na-Gig that is on the wall at Killnaboy, in County Clare, Ireland.

Is the Sheela-na-Gig a representation of a displaced godhead from an earlier pre-Christian religion? For me she represents – with her grimace, her ribs showing, and her open vulva – a goddess of both life and death.

Many people turn more naturally to a goddess figure, however they understand her, for help when in need. So this poem is included in the hope it might express the feelings of those who relate to this female spiritual force in the natural and supernatural world.

Little Goddess

stronger than death for us
small and tall for us
holding life open for us
living not dying for us
young and old for us
invisible and huge for us
mirth and tears for us
bone and blood for us
warm and cold for us
dark and light for us
small and tough for us
strong for us
young for us
there for us
what prayer for us
shelter from the cold for us
old for us
bold and brass for us
laugh and alive for us
last for us
too much for us
too big for us
stronger than life for us
have love for us

Small Goddess

THE KIND PROVIDER

Grief *is* the kind provider, because without it we cannot find ease with life again. But some griefs are too acute. This poem came to me when I had witnessed the huge loss a young woman suffered when her young husband died, completely unexpectedly, of an asthma attack.

They happened to be deep in the country and help did not get to him in time. They were living a blissfully happy life, fulfilled and contented, doing the work they enjoyed. She told me they had just had the happiest year of their lives. There is no answer to this.

There are deaths that should not have happened; the timing is wrong and we are horrified by it. However, we have no choice but to face it. And yet, if we manage to access our deep sources of grief and allow them expression – however difficult this is – we will be open to true relief and the strength to move on.

In the past here in Ireland there would be professional keeners at a funeral who would sing formal laments for the dead. They tended on the whole to be women, and they cried out in a particular wailing song to express people's grief.

We belong to a less demonstrative culture now, which is not necessarily a good thing. Emotions demand to be expressed. We should not hold back our expressions of grief, and I can see that keening was a dramatic and formal recognition of this truth.

The Kind Provider

There is no mantle I can lay down
no comfort I can pull from the hedgerows.

Grief looks out with his plain stare

then goes around the corner, knows
we can only take him by degrees.
Knows he is needed. That he has to come
but not at once. First Brother Shock
paralyses with his mute needle.

So on goes the body, mind, heart,
tick tock, doing, doing,
managing and ordering this and that.
Grief waits until asked,
is appalling and healthy.

Grief waters the gardens in the night-time.

With grief, we can find a pathway.
Grief kindly provides a river.

HEART'S BLOOD

On the death of a child

What can anyone say about the death of a very young child, any child? It is impossible to speak about this loss. How to console someone who has suffered this? We are struck dumb by the enormity of their loss. We can't help feeling deep relief that we have not to face such a fate. I suppose we can feel that at least the small child has been spared most of the pains and difficulties of life. But it faces us with the reality that life, however difficult, is a gift, and then consoles us with the fact that a life however short has its own truth, reality and perfection.

It is those left behind who have to struggle to come to terms with their loss, and try to celebrate the brief life of the child in the best and fullest way they can. This poem is an attempt to express the loss of the new young life which is, to us, perfection.

Heart's Blood

On the death of a child

        Beloved,
you left too early

 you could not rest
you took wing
 you fled the world

perfect in all things

 your bright eyes
your hair of down
 your brief breath

your faultless limbs
 your white feet
your nails of blossom −

 O my great love for you

I would cradle you
 rock you forever
send soft dreams to you

the milk not dry on your mouth −

Joy and fun for you
 send you love and laughing
pleasure and plenty
 kindness and kisses that

71

you will never be empty,
  heart shielded now
from cruelty and snare.
  I would always be there.

May you live in
warmlight
    in kind gardens
      with soft air
with light, loves, birds,
  doves – animals to
    play with you

      love above you
      love below you
      love around you
      love to know you

Wrapped in love will you be

  for all this great eternity.

    My little one
    my loved one
  My own heart's blood.
    My dear darling.

THE SEAL

I'm watching two trees that stand in the road outside my house. I see them from my window as I write: one is a London plane and the other a lime. Each is distinct and has its own life pattern, shedding and growing its new leaves at different times. The plane is nearer to the house, and has an irritating habit of losing some leaves all the year around: this means my front garden is never free of fallen leaves. When its time comes, and the sap no longer holds the leaf to its branch, each and every leaf has its time to drop, spiralling down in a beautiful gentle movement, choosing the moment the sap ceases, the leaf lets go.

It is said that we don't choose our moment to die, but is this really true? When my dear mother-in-law was in hospital in England, I got over to see her before my husband, who was her youngest and remaining son, was able to do so. She was in her nineties; she was very frail and not expected to last. I arrived and was visiting her every day. She became very much better, and was sitting up in a chair by the time her son arrived. We shared a good time, all three of us together. Then we left and I had only arrived home in the door the same evening when the hospital phoned to say she had died.

Of course the death of a child is not the same as that of a woman who has lived fully through a long life. Yet all leavings reflect that simple fall of the leaf.

I suppose that is the task we are set when we deal with death, our own or another's, in whatever form we meet it. Acceptance is difficult because it means what it says: it is a kind of giving in, a passivity not an action, and it can seem easier to act rather than to be still and accept.

The Seal

God given life
God given death

You give one
take the other

if you are the good God
I must accept your decision

that coming
this going.

I watch the gold discs –
the leaves who wait their time –
a casual breeze
seals their fate

the sweet juice
closed from them
then the final flight –
the drop to abyss.

My little one's breath
left never to return.

There is no stillness
as a child's stillness.

A deep coldness
seals my fate.

STILL

At least, now, we can and do talk about losses that in the past were hidden in the most appalling silence.

I was twelve years old before I had any idea, even an inkling, that my parents had lost stillborn full-term twin daughters, five years before my own birth. My mother spoke of it to me just once, I was about twelve, I wept, I think she was so shocked at my upset and it was never mentioned again. I was never able to speak of it to her or my father. Both parents died in my early adulthood; somehow, the time was not ready for the subject to be aired.

Later on, an aunt, my mother's sister could fill in a little. She had seen their little bodies, and how perfect they were, she told me how anxious my mother was that they would be baptised, my mother was very ill with tox-aemia and lucky to survive. One question arose, where were they buried. How strange this seems, that I do not know. I was told they would have been put into the coffins of some other dead and buried with them. So somewhere, in some graveyard near my family's home, my stillborn sisters lie with strangers. There must be many families who have equally difficult stories. I wrote the poem "Still" to commemorate these sisters of mine, to acknowledge their brief womb life and, in a way bury them. Nowadays these losses are acknowledged, expressed, and the unborn infants given their place, and their burial.

Still

The dead await you.
Their cold arms
Their still minds
Are open

Where do my stillborn sisters lie
Orphaned in another's grave?
Did they lay you side by side
Curved, womb moulded naturally?

Little moon
children,
secure
on a tendril,
you float
tied
to the side
of the world.

Playing
in your warm
dawn,
rocked
by your great
sea mother,
drops
in her fertile ocean.

Heartbeat
Heartbeat
repeat
the certainty
of the other.

Pale plantings
your sun
surrounds,
engorged
with plenty
knowing
each shove and showing
touch and tread
in your cosy country.

What   that
sharp   cry
where   beyond
is   there?
Out   there
this   light
night   descending
where sister where
this   downing
An abyss
an outer space
place?
O no place.

They lay upon the table
they were perfect   she said
perfect with hair and shell nails
and tiny eyes.   They lay on the table
in the bright light perfect
their toes curled in mild
surprise at being there.

While my mother fought to live
Tempest tossed upon her bed
In another women's arms
Her sweet fruits were laid to rest.

The gentle dead encompass you
Nothing new can harm or snare
You who never felt a breath
Perfect in the earthing's care.

The dead await you.
Their cold breasts
Their still minds
Are open,
And the earth is blind.

HARVEST: THE SISTER

This is another poem from *Now is a Moveable Feast*.

It is based on the true story of a young woman, my grandmother's sister Lily, who died in childbirth, as did her child, because she did not have the appropriate medical help. Fortunately, this is a rare happening nowadays.

In the poem I use the story in Luke's Gospel about Elizabeth visiting her cousin Mary when they both were pregnant, to mirror my grandmother's love and concern for her sister and her unborn child.

Elizabeth and Mary, once they were delivered, would have brought their newborn child to present him to God in the Temple, and brought also an offering of turtledoves in thanksgiving for a safe birth. Of course in the real life story my grandmother's sister would have had no use for the turtledoves, as there was no child to present, so the doves could fly free.

The quotation from Matthew's Gospel is itself a quotation from the words of Jeremiah in the Old Testament, which Matthew sees as a prophecy of the Massacre of the Innocents. Matthew tells us that Herod, the King of Judea, was perturbed when he heard from the Three Wise Men about the birth of a new King of the Jews.

When he feared that the child might escape his grasp, he ordered the killing of all male infants in the city of Bethlehem under the age of two. But Joseph had been warned of the danger in a dream; so he and Mary and the child Jesus fled into neighbouring Egypt and were saved.

The death of a child produces a tumult of emotions, one of which is that these innocent ones have been cheated of life. We may also feel that we have let the child down by not being able to save them.

Harvest: The Sister

'rising up in those days
went into the country
with haste'

LUKE 1:39

Sister Sister
  never more
Will your winsome
  infant leap

Hear the knock
  upon the door
Hear the coming
  of my feet,

Bring O bring no turtledoves.

How you spoke
  with love to me
Of your growing
  family,

You who bore him
  daughters, sons,
Left to die in
  childbirth pangs.

Bring O bring no turtledoves.

     Smooth down
     Smooth down
     Dear Mother

The pale cold sheet she said,

Kneel down
Kneel down
Dear daughter

Close, by your sister's head,

Listen
My dear
O listen,

The song I sang is dead.

Bring O bring no turtledoves.

The child that curls
inside her,

Is carved
And still
As stone.

Pray on
Pray on
Dear daughter

For my heart is lost and gone.

O bring no turtledoves

She sang
O so sang she:

My babe and I
Are bound to die,

So let the doves fly free.

THE GIFT OF FREEDOM

The tradition in our islands, Ireland and Britain, has long been to bury the dead. This custom has changed, and quite rapidly here in Ireland: it is now just as common here as in Britain to have a cremation. Because of this, we need new prayers or poems and songs, to incorporate different imagery. So the next two poems are for the scattering or burial of ashes following a cremation.

The scattering of ashes enables us to leave the remains of the dead in beautiful places, at places perhaps that were particularly loved by them. This opens new possibilities. Burial at sea is one alternative, or to scatter ashes on the waves of some magnificent beach. The giving of our dead to the waves, to the air, to a river – to the natural world – is liberating.

We all have special landscapes, personal places that we love. Then we have a place to go back to where we remember those we have lost, a place to lay flowers; to pause, remember and reflect.

The Gift of Freedom

Poem for the scattering of ashes to the air, land and sea.

This is: our giving away

to the winds
to the air
up, light and free
not left with one care

sailing into the heavens
falling on the earth
what was death
is now changed to birth.

The growing green take you
the tree's leaves enwrap you
the stream swift you
the rich earth for you

the sea's depths for you
the ocean's breath for you
the clean salt for you
the fast rocks for you
the free sail for you
the keen wind for you

the whole heavens for you
the deep depths for you
the high skies for you
the stars for you

our prayers go with you, but
our minds keep you with us
rest deep within us
you go – though never leave us
you leave – but stay with us

You stay in the swirling light
you stay in the night's dark
you stay in the kindness of friends
you stay at the shared meal
you stay in the wine's depths
you stay by the warming fire

you stay in our quiet talks
you stay in stories told
you stay in our laughter
you stay in our home's shelter.

In the long grass of summer
may you lie down with comfort

given to the skies
laid down on the earth
it is by passing through death –
we are open for birth.

INTO THE WIND

This is another poem rather in the same vein as the one before. Both the choices – to end in the earth, or by fire and air – are positive, and part of creation. We who are still here, and part of someone else's leaving, celebrate them as whole-heartedly as possible.

I remember with a feeling of warmth and joy the scattering of ashes of a dear friend, which took place on a small beach in the west of Ireland. This is a beach that I use often in the summer.

This friend had died suddenly, and too young. I went with her husband and grown-up children to the beach where they were to throw her ashes into the sea. They sang a favourite song of hers, then her husband and son jumped out into the waves and cast her ashes out on the waters. It was moving, intimate and beautiful. One of the reasons the family had chosen this small beach was that their wife and mother had been particularly happy in this place. The other was that her homeland was America. The Atlantic Ocean touches the shores of both Ireland and America, so throwing her ashes into those waters connected her with both her countries

I must admit I was afraid that when I returned to this little beach, which I do often on holiday, that I would remember – and be sad. But no, it is the opposite in fact – I feel happy and warmed remembering. Good and surprising things can come from going boldly through mourning in the way that is right for you.

Into The Wind

for scattering of ashes

i

You have chosen to go
in the clean flames to the skies
as we here below remember
our times together.

We salute you for choosing
the wild way of wind.

No cold earth for you
no deep grave
no stone to mark
your name to save.

You chose the brightness
the leaping light flame
so there on the breeze
ashes scatter your name.

And into this All
you become fully one.
Tossed into the free air
new life begun.

When I set a match to a fire
when flames fill the grate
and warm, like a pyre
sending sparks to the heavens

as you have chosen to go
in clear flames to the skies
and your friends here below
remember shared times.

ii

To the warm air
the bright skies
to the white clouds
to the wave's eye

to the tall trees
to the fresh grass
with the drone of bees
on a mountains path

in the gull's soar
to the hawk's stoop
to the stage's roar
to the swallow's loop

in the rivers swell
in the sea's tides
in the dropping rain
in the wind's glide.

DREAM

I have always felt that celebrating is a most important part of life. That we should celebrate frequently, and make good times, and look forward. That we can, if we try, fulfil our own dreams. That it is good and fun to throw troubles to the winds and rejoice.

Shakespeare always gave great place to the Fool in his plays. The Fool could say with impunity what was not permitted to others. That was his job, to point out to the King his weak spots, to 'send things up' as we say. My Father always said if he had not been a doctor he would have been a clown, he had a wonderful lively sense of humour. Also I was also lucky at school that the nuns were great at making our feast days – and there were many of them – the greatest fun. I think both my Father and the nuns inspired me all my life to have love-ly family celebrations, and good parties. I love parties.

I do think it is wise to be foolish. The poet is free to say the unsayable if she or he is worth her salt. I do not think joy lands on our plates; it is up to us to make it. This is a poem celebrating wildness, to say it's fun and good to go a bit mad, to kick up our heels.

Dream

Let our dreams be mad
  why else should we be dreaming
It's easy to be sad,
  planning, thinking, scheming

Let wildness have its play
  the dancing and the singing
Joy make out our day
  unreason do the ringing

Fools have the better half
  the truer and the richer
Pressed down and running over
  fill up the empty pitcher

Sweet wine of life dance on
  keep the pulse a-beating
And when I dance to death
  oh let me keep on dreaming.

WEIGHING THINGS UP

I quite often think of my own death, and how will things go on afterwards. I imagine I will see and know everything, like a fly on the wall, watching – but I really have no idea.

However, a thought came to me that I found most consoling, and it makes great sense: that dying is the last loving act we do for our children.

Why do I say that? Because we clear a space for them, we remove from their shoulders the responsibilities they have to us. We present them with a different freedom. It may be a lonely freedom at times, but natural and therefore good.

My mother died when I was expecting my first child. I was in my very early twenties, and she died three months before the baby's birth, so I was denied a truly adult relation with my mother, and my children lost a loving grandmother. So perhaps because of the timing of my mother's death, birth and death are always related in my mind. I have found out too, decades later, that the birth of my son had covered up my grief, so it was only twenty five years later that I managed to grieve properly.

But I also remember a sense of relief at her death, which of course made me feel guilty. We always feel we have not done enough when our closest ones die. So this poem is to my adult children, hoping to relieve them of guilt, hoping they will enjoy their freedom, so that they will be able to grieve well, and not be burdened.

I love our Irish custom that the men of the family carry the coffin on their shoulders to the grave, or nowadays to the cremation. So, as their mother who carried them to birth, I may be carried by my sons to the next life.

Weighing Things Up

Four Sons to Carry My Coffin

I will be the last weight on your shoulders
the groove of wood cutting down on your bone
you carry my dust to its earth, or fire, or water
anyway to some distant horizon that exists or
                    does not exist

Never more will you know that pressure of
Motherhood upon you. You as well as I are released
from my time with all its responsibilities. Never fret
take time, smile, be happy. The simple clichés
                    are best

We know but never expect we will come to this.
Dying is love. Very practical. I am taking my time,
                    and moving on.

About the Author

Anne Le Marquand Hartigan is an award-winning poet, play-wright and painter. She trained as a painter at Reading University, England. She returned to Co Louth, Ireland, in 1962 with her husband Tim Hartigan where they farmed and reared their six children. She now lives in Dublin.

To Keep The Light Burning is her sixth collection of poetry, fol-lowing *Nourishment* (Salmon, 2005), *Immortal Sins* (Salmon, 1993) and *Now is a Moveable Feast* (1991), an award-winning long poem with Anne's drawings. *Return Single* (1986) and *Long Tongue* (1982) were both published by Beaver Row Press, Dublin. Her prose work includes *Clearing The Space, the Why of Writing*, published in 1996 by Salmon.

Hartigan won the Mobil Prize for Playwriting for her play *The Secret Game* in 1995. *In Other Worlds* (2003) was commissioned and performed by Ohio University, USA, then performed at the Edinburgh Fringe Festival and Otago, Dunedin, New Zealand. *Jersey Lilies* performed at the Samuel Beckett Theatre, Dublin, in 1996, with Anne acting alongside Robert Gordon in this two-hander. *La Corbiere* performed at the Project Theatre during the Dublin Theatre Festival of 1989, and since then has been performed in Beirut (2004), by Solas Nua Theatre Company in Washington DC (July 2006), and in venues throughout Ireland. Her first play, *Beds* at the Damer Theatre, was part of the Dublin Theatre Festival in 1982. *La Corbiere* is published in *SeenandHeard: six new plays by Irish Women*, edited by Cathy Leeney and published in 2001 by Carysfort Press, Dublin.

Anne has widely exhibited her paintings, batiks and installa-tions, for which she has won awards, in Ireland and the UK, with one woman, two person and in major national group shows.